The hoop

JOHN BURNSIDE
The Hoop

CARCANET

For Sheila

Acknowledgement is due to the editors of the following journals in which some poems from this collection first appeared: *Encounter*, *Orbis*, *PN Review*, and *Poetry Durham*.

First published in 1988 by
Carcanet Press Limited
208-212 Corn Exchange Buildings
Manchester M4 3BQ

Copyright © 1988 John Burnside
All rights reserved

British Library Cataloguing in Publication Data

Burnside, John
  The hoop.
  I. Title
  821'.914   PR6052.U668/

ISBN 0-85635-742-1

The publisher acknowledges financial assistance from
the Arts Council of Great Britain

Typeset in 10pt Palatino by Bryan Williamson, Manchester
Printed in England by SRP Ltd, Exeter

Contents

1 *The hoop*

Mandelstam at Voronezh	9
Psyche-Life	11
Lazarus	12
Vallejo	13
'That game of finding'	14
'The way the dead'	15
'Silence is possible'	16
Looking glass winter	17
Leaving Nutwood	18
Victoriana	19
The myth of Narcissus	24
Fever	25
After Viking	26
Naked	27
Inside	28
Tundra's edge	29
Runners	30
Leavings	31
Ursa Major	32
Us	33
Two	34
Eumenides	35
The hoop	37

2 *Green*

Green	43
El búho	44
Taking Sheila to the zoology museum	45
Nature study	46
Aide mémoire	47
Lost	48
Out of exile	49
Exile's return	50
Personal	51
Keeping secret	53
Clarity	54

Brother	55
Two saints	56
A death in the family	58
Silentium	59
Fetching sloes	60
Self-	61
Anamnesis	62
The quest	63
'Only the rain'	68
The bounds	69
All Hallows at Newbrook Farm	72
After the harvest	73
Green	74
An English Suite	75

1

The hoop

Mandelstam at Voronezh

1

So you stood in the yellow street
with memory strapped to your face
like a diver's lung:

chocolate, the feel of silk,
fragments of requiem.

Your beggar-woman friend
waited by the stove
with blueberry stains
on her blue hands

and you stood in the yellow street
with song like a juice on your lips
freezing already, as blackbirds whispered

Quest'è l'verno, ma tal, che gioia apporte.

2

There is a face in the whitest
corner of the frost:
half-bear, half-featureless, and almost
human, like the face
of any accident;

something you simply endured, as fish
endure their sleeves of ice,
swollen lines, whispered for years
to walls, to the ten-figured forests,
scratched on the winter's vellum,

almost word-perfect. No birds
at the station gates, but the face
was there: you spoke its name
before the train moved out and frost
settled on your lips and on your hands.

Psyche-Life

The soul is a woman perhaps.
Or else a dialect,
the local variation of
a common tongue. So she remains
six days in the city of roots
surrounded by strange voices.
She eats the sickly food.
On the seventh day she returns;
the moon dissolves in a blue milk
above a vineyard.
The earth is netted in song.
The soul is a dialect, perhaps.
Or else: a woman, coming home
from mildew to a new
household of objects that shine,
mirrors and lozenges,
trifles of copper and silk.

Lazarus

A cry in the village of doves:
cold water swings like a bell
in a stone jar; behind each door
the elders crouch in shadow
reciting genealogies
or numbering possessions.
The body is still. It sweats.
Even in the sepulchre
there are perfumes and birdsong,
there is the memory of touch
like a fingerprint on the soul,
and outside, in the garden:
water and leaves, enactment,
the discipline of waking.

Vallejo

Me moriré en París con aguacero

I dreamed of you in Paris:

you opened a door and stepped in from the rain
and you were standing in the hallway of
the eternal Thursday where all the dead
wait in their rented rooms;

you smelled the wax and burning vegetables
and the stale rain in your winter coat
as you climbed the stairs of
the eternal Thursday; ten francs

paid in advance to lie down
in your cold suit of hunger
beside mother and brothers and tortured bulls
in the long bed of the eternal Thursday

in the Paris of dreams where bleeding angels
hover like flies in the drapery of rain.

'That game of finding'

That game of finding someone in the house,
of stopping dead and listening for steps
behind a door. Only a game,
until the make-believe insinuates
a form. Or I pretend
something has just melted from the room
when I walk in, sensing the pinprick chill
of kindred skin.
The walls have voices, clear
singsong through the fallow afternoon,
leaving me to denser silences
where something grows, larger than I would choose
and moving, of its own accord,
towards me, fast becoming teeth and eyes.

'The way the dead'

The way the dead are familiar,
looking for empty spaces to
hold them, as the people in your dreams
are always climbing or falling;

how they keep appearing, like weeds
in herbaceous borders: moleskin
figures amongst the lupins,
nodding and waving. They treat your moths

as angels; they leave kid gloves
and feathers in the kitchen,
or come in suddenly at dusk,
expecting tea. The way they flit

from house to house in long
processions of hatstands and mirrors;
how they sit in the public parks,
playing draughts. Or how a doorway fills

around you in a rainstorm
and, too late, you know who they are,
with their blue smiles and mottled bodies
shuffling, pressing closer, making room.

'Silence is possible'

Silence is possible, and after dark
it almost happens: silence, like a glove,
the perfect fit you always hoped to find.
But somewhere close a child is whimpering;
like the sound of a backstreet violin
the wind is everywhere, repetitive
and incomplete. Sirens are wailing
all over the city. New snow creaks
under leather. Silence is possible,
but you have been a listener for years
and what could you find but the hard quiet
of huddled swimmers in a riverbed
or the casual hush of abattoirs
after the thud of a bullet nobody heard.

Looking glass winter

The hedge is straighter there, expressed as snow,
bright rooves and turning lanes
measured and sure. We are content to see
the stillness deepen, and the slow
wheel of pigeons is the more controlled
for being silent. This could be a world
of perfect balance: each quicksilver line
bridles the shuddering wave of what would rise
above its element, and we appear
only by chance, unless our looks confine
the surge that would replace us with surprise
when horses break the surface of the glass,
supple and heavy, dancing to the clear
borderline of substance and thin air.

Leaving Nutwood

On the veranda, talk of other years
and other weathers: not since forty-six
was summer as unbearable as this.
Voices fall for wasted birthday gifts,
for details of a stranger's patient death
and words like *cancer*, sharp under the breath.

In Nutwood, history repeats itself
forever. Chinese palaces exist
behind red doors and on a dusty shelf
Rupert finds a key. Life is a mist
where there is always something else to find.
And no one leaves, though all are left behind.

Magpies rattle out above the trees.
I used to hear them on the way to school.
One year a dead bird rotted on our hill
for days. The wings were animate with fleas.
The worm casts on the lawn smell dark and fresh:
what are they but flaked knucklebones and flesh?

In picture stories no one ever dies
and no one whispers. Bright amidst the leaves
red berries are a promise of clean snow
and children wading home in boots and scarves.
All summer long the woods are full of tracks
but safety always hobbles at our backs.

On the veranda, someone strikes a match
and sunlight blisters in a reef of smoke.
I feel the story slipping out of reach,
a page lost when I put away the book.
In Nutwood, Rupert sets out with his friends
for new adventures, where my childhood ends.

Victoriana

1

We came through webs of hunger
to leaf fires by the hedge,
lost in a stranger's language,
in a garden of unreal flowers:

white dresses on the parterre,
Crown Derby and clotted cream,
summer's indelible shadows
at croquet on the lawn.

Hidden in the rat paths,
black-eyed among the alders,
we saw their Christmas trees
in deep bay windows

and nursery faces answered,
children in spotless linen
between the floral curtains,
watching their night for claws.

2

When the candlesticks were bandaged,
when the parlour smelled of old wax
and men in black coats at the door
led us towards black horses,

when I held my breath and the rain
continued for days, when strangers
gathered in the rooms with loud cups and
slow conversation, I thought

of marbled books and hyacinths,
and places I must have seen
on visits: empty provinces

where men played hide-and-seek with bones,
and the dead became their portraits,
filling the halls with history and trust.

3

A tree falls and nobody sees.
And no one sees our moving hands
behind a floral curtain,
or the pictures we sometimes find
in bureau drawers.
Nobody tells us secrets:
we stand by the graves in silence,
we listen at doors, bewildered,
we rob a pigeons' nest to hold
the eggs in our wet mouths.
Trees fall and no one sees;
but God sees, to make it happen.
And we see night moths on the glass
and dust on our hands from killing.

4

Four lost in so many years,
drowned heads in narrow boxes,
glass eyes under the turf.
No one is stronger than the dead

children who were neither seen nor heard
when a dropped coal flared to the scalp,
boot-blacks with gangrenous fractures,
match girls caught in wheels.

Between the stone ship and the gate,
between the yew hedge and the house of rest,
yellow curls and charcoal muslins
gleamed in the opaline sunlight.

We thought they would guide our lives
from charitable sleep,
but, catching us unawares, they exacted
a skipping song's revenge.

5

Where white doves have made a dovecote
of the burnt-out wing of a house
and monkshood grows beside a wall,
the fretted soot and indigo
are doorways to an ideal place
that might have happened. Where the sun
intrudes upon the weasel's kill
we find the secret garden:
blood and lilac, leaf and bone,
looking-glass loves and murders,
and here, where the door is bolted,
a promise of things left undone.

The myth of Narcissus

In that world I was alone.
Elsewhere, there was a blur of tents,
the coloured rags of others. Voices
splashed towards me through the fox-red
bracken, but I never recognised
the names they gave,
and nothing happened there until
my fingers broke the surface and
by water I began to understand,
not the reflected, but the fact
of being seen. Then the trees were real.
Sunlight found each leaf.
Presence arrived in ripples at my skin.

Fever

There would be substance in a thread
of water; sure identity
in drinking. Ribbons of sweat
curl from the palm of a stranger
who slept in your bed overnight;
crocuses flare on the lawn
like tapers of purple dew; sunlight
drifts along a ditch like willow down.
Imagine the worst dream: kissing bone
under a stone floor and hearing
your own steps pace the surface.
Imagine an alien fever, satisfied
hereafter: someone drinking in your place,
parched lips and fingers pressed to frosted glass.

After Viking

The feel of an empty world:
grey promenade, grey slate,
ash-grey fog fuzzing window panes.

Our colour is the foxing in old books,
the lime-green possibility
of life in space

but form is the sub-organic
hoop of the virus.
Empty rooms, cold eggs, forgotten wounds

opening along the back and thighs.
Our music is a bottle full of wasps
and aching seas

but silence is the choice we failed to make:
the body's hidden net of weightlessness
and spectral lichens on the crust of Mars.

Naked

Imagine us really naked. We never are.
Even in private we clothe ourselves
with one another, with the thought of love.
Alone, I search for hidden animals
on the tight skin of the mirror:
the callous, muscular bear of me who feeds
on honey and blood; the bird of paradise;
the sweet-faced jackal sniffing at the glass.
Eventually I find a lizard
nakedness, and this is hard to take:
nothing I would show to someone else,
not even you. Yet going dressed –
one seeming member of a seemly world –
I am single and sure, and naked to the bone.

Inside

Spiders wheel on wires; a night bird
calls; like the pain in our hands
the dripping never stops and only
someone else would say it was the loose
washer in a tap. We know this house:
we know it locked to water and the snow;
even the lawn, the laurels and whited spruce
are seen through glass, a crystal ornament
we cannot break. Sometimes we feel the wind
against a door; sometimes we speak
of kinship with the dark, but never step
beyond the patio, and night is best
appreciated in this hoop of light
where dripping is and everybody knows
magic is somewhere else, where no one goes.

Tundra's edge

Here is the wolf. The wind, the sound of rain,
the kitchen light that falls across the lawn –
these things are his. This house is his domain.

Here is the wolf. He slips in with the dawn
to raid your mirrors. Shadows will persist
for days, to mark the distance he has gone

in search of you. Yet still you will insist
the wolf died out in these parts long ago:
everyone knows the wolf does not exist.

You catch no scent. And where the mirrors glow
those are not eyes, but random sparks of light.
You never dream of running with the snow.

Yet here is Wolf. He rustles in the night.
Only the wind, but you switch on the light.

Runners

In these late days, early enough to mourn
the tragedy of the commons, late enough
not to do much about it, we begin
making strange lists: the diverse sounds of winds,
the words in Eskimo for snow, the names
of those who die in infancy. And some,
learning the furtive ways of bear or fox,
vanish within themselves. We have been lost
in our own house for years. Now we go out
at morning and we run – not to be fit
and not to win: there are no victories,
but on our way the trees are full of rain,
children deliver papers in the dark,
fear makes things real. We live, and we may see
the end. No exercise is futile now.

Leavings

Perhaps they will open a coffin somewhere else,
spilling the contents over a barren field
where broken stones had been, and charcoal wings.
Scraping the fingers, black beneath the rings,

cutting back a green that is not moss,
perhaps they will find, in coils around the spine,
a rag of yellow linen, stiff with bile,
or pollen in the hair, or eglantine,

and this will be the salvage they require:
one seed-pod in the lining of a coat,
the unconsidered cargo of old grain,
to sow fresh pastures in the first clean rain.

Ursa Major

We live against the silence of
imagined bears, against
stillness, like a tarpaulin of snow
laid on fur, against the tang
of isolation, sharp as juniper.
There are old sweetnesses
remembered through the wind, dark
huckleberries cracking on the tongue
and feral honey, there are
stillbirths and sprung traps yet,
lost scents and the unexpected
echo in the stars of what we thought
was random discontent
and flawed delight.

Us

This is what ought to be:
blue street, milk float,
the smell of ink and grain.

Nothing soothes the eye
as walls and fences do,
speckled with lilac rain

or snow-ridged, in
the seeping dawn.
Nothing soothes us more
than hedges and doors

and the sense of ourselves
as secret rooms,
deep in the one house,
busy with space and time.

Two

He was growing old in the sound of water,
the smell of heat and sheet webs in the grass;
he was changing with the good names in his throat:
the mystery of *bear*, the shock of *mouse*.

She must have been the owl beneath his lung,
the thought of darkness swelling in the bone.
But when he homed in her, he found a gap
and like the snake he slithered through alone.

Eumenides

1

As if they could have been renamed
by mortals. Slugs come up for rain; the sky
bruises; formless, piecemeal,
they surface to the old

condition: water smell, the colour black, the sense
reptile. You shelter them
unwittingly, beneath wet eaves and tiles; they touch you
daily, at eyelid and groin, their soiled

fingertips a harnessing by feel,
or hidden in the looking glass, they peel
a thick, warm film of tallow from your skin,
where bloated scales are plucked, plumes grafted in.

2

This is the mistake you learn by heart:
the wrong word for the wrong
reason; wet-mouthed
rancour, sweetened by naming.

Slowly, the fog stiffens. Dogs
whimper in the yard; hard
spectres reappear: fiends splashed in mould,
cold hosts exhumed from crusts of blood and gold.

Black water in the roof. Black drifts of seed.
You slide against a wall of feathered stone
and talons. They have come for you alone.
Their grip is sure, complicit with the bone.

The hoop

The nation's hoop is broken and scattered. There is no centre any longer and the sacred tree is dead.
                                          Black Elk

1

Someone was walking in the room next door.
I thought the house was empty but it seems
someone was pacing round the bedroom floor

a moment since. His footsteps crossed my dreams
as I was waking; sunlight bleached the wall,
and on the other side it must have gleamed

upon his space. Each step rang hard and small:
a slow, deliberate measurement of pain.
At times these old, familiar sounds appal,

at times it seems the morning light is strained
from utter blackness. Yet I bear it all:
the scattered hoop, the poison in the grain,

and naked angels, shattered in the fall.
My own steps echo in an empty hall.

2

We say it cannot happen now. It does.
Executives with chainsaw eyes dictate
a blond security. I almost hear the buzz

of torture offices, as telepriests relate
my enmities to shadows who fulfil
a need for darkness in the perfect state.

Where Destiny is Manifest, I kill
by proxy, but I profit from the dead.
Focussed on the screen, I see no ill;

my lack of vision buys two loaves of bread.
Or I protest: my terms are redefined
and filtered back, distorting what was said,

until imagination is confined
and small clichés creep easily to mind.

3

Quite often, momentarily, I think
an angel is imprisoned in this wall.
I sense its presence, liquid, bright as ink,

by day I sometimes hear its siren call
to others of the tribe: it sings of night
and sweet white dust in nurseries and halls

where humans seal their angels up for spite.
Yet angels might be demons; their disguise
is of my making. Shadows breed from light

and veil things with significance; my eyes
are echo chambers where the seraphim
are plucked of meaning, as creation dies.

And if the feathers burn beneath my skin
I hold my breath to keep the devil in.

4

Hern. I only heard the word used once
and yet it echoes down the tunneled years.
I search in books for a significance

books do not give, although the word appears
in lexicons: *Old English, secret place*
or corner, (rare, obscure).
                    Whenever darkness stains

my skin with history, or tracks my face
with freezing water, this word seems a key
and, breathless in the labyrinth, I trace

a thread between one wall that seems to me
extended randomly to hide the night,
and something else that almost fails to be

turned in upon itself and, knotted tight,
centres the hoop and makes a hern of light.

5

The dark is welling up. It fills my hand
with freezing seed. In here, I stand alone.
The lights are out. I do not understand

and silence hardens in my throat like bone.
The hoop is scattered now, and yet I know
the tree is rooted in the broken stone.

Beneath my fingernails, new feathers glow
– we say the angel cannot be contained –
within the circle of the dark I grow:

imperfect, whole, the green of me sustained
by blackness at the core. I spell things out:
from utter silence every word is strained.

And when the hidden devil longs to shout
I open up and breathe the angel out.

2

Green

Green

You never lose it. Never.
You buy a new clearwater looking glass
and two years afterwards it's green

like windows in old houses where the trees
echo in each pane, or the old pond
beyond the garden, shot with blanket grass.

You never lose it. Even in your dreams
you find convolvulus and dyer's weed
and poison daisy. You have simazine,

gramoxone, diquat, in the garden shed.
You purify the water; everything
is bleached and sterilised.

Still it persists. The path you scrubbed with lye
had olive demons etched in the cement.
No time at all before they grow again.

El búho

From the Spanish, búho: *nm 1. owl. 2. inf. hermit.*

At midnight I am hunting on the clock's
white face. I move between numbers,
timed to perfection, like a second hand.
I crunch mice in the wheel house of the dark;
my skin learns feathers, memory
is a wooden room with a cord, and no way out.
At midnight I am innocent as milk,
intimate with shadows, pressed
against the crystal: fingers, nostrils, tongue
finding semen in the smell of wax
and veins in the pendulum. Time
muffles my speech like fur, and I am cracked
wafer and bone, fluttering in the springs,
heavy with dust and flightless, flightless and blind.

Taking Sheila to the zoology museum

Look. This fish is frozen in a net
of formalin. The eyes are little stones.
Within each jar a history has set

like jam, or wax; we trace the numbered bones
through aniline; the ligaments and nerves
are nicely finished; everything is shown.

We get the evolution we deserve:
instructive, clearly-labelled, in its place.
We keep dead letters. Nobody preserves

random flight, the variables of grace,
the animation nothing could suspend.
But on the landing, in an unmarked case,

like some dark feast that time could not attend,
a lungfish dreams to no apparent end.

Nature study

You keep such talismans as contradict
social expectations:
tiny bones, a common lizard's skull,
one patch of diamond skin across the crown

worn thin, as if by rain.
You press dead leaves: the colouring will fade
year by year, but autumn may persist
between the books. And butterflies,

when pinned on setting boards shed yellow scales,
their tinsel, poisoned memoirs
of the net. The things you kill
may lend security on troubled nights,

labelled with the catechismal names
or studied by a desk lamp after dark
to memorise a pattern: marbled veins
or hairstreaks. Talismans are claimed

when fear outweighs community of sense;
another fool might rush
headlong, empty-handed, at the world
and perish uselessly,

you stay at home. A wing is all it takes
to cancel the disorder that intrudes,
and ranks of tense antennae, ridged with hairs,
defend your space against all predators.

Aide mémoire

It was hidden under shells and feathers:
something she had found in curls of sand,
some bitter relic of another time,
of headlong thrushes hanging from a tree,
concertina wings, eyes stitched with lime.

No name for it, though yellow fossil hairs
crept in the seams, and threads of malachite
glittered in the cracks.
It could have been a piece of yellow glass,
a splintered bone, a ball of sealing wax.

And no name for the angel, or the boys
who sneaked into her dreams with knives and fire:
all she knew was bad, and after prayers
the buried keepsakes rattled in the dark
beneath her papers dolls and Chinese squares.

Lost

The fog walks down the hill and finds our yard:
curious, like a tourist, filling up
corners, measuring spaces, rescuing
mystery from the commonplace. We take
no little pride in our slight membership
of this all-knowing whiteness; echoes fall
two yards away and plunge into the deep
beside us, like the voices in a well,
and home was unremarkable until
it disappeared into the hinterland
behind our practised blindness, where we keep
private forests, mountains, shifting sands
on lucid, instinct maps of holy ground
we render to the fog when we are found.

Out of exile

When we are driving through the border towns
we talk of houses, empty after years
of tea and conversation;
of afternoons marooned against a clock
and silences elected out of fear,
of lives endured for what we disbelieved.

We recognise the shop fronts and the names,
the rushing trees and streets into the dark;
we recognise a pattern in the sky:
blackness flapping like a broken tent,
shadow foxes running in the stars.
But what we recognise is what we bring.

Driving, early, through the border towns,
the dark stone houses clanging at our wheels,
and we invent things as they might have been:
a light switched on, some night, against the cold,
and children at the door, with bags and coats,
telling stories, laughing, coming home.

Exile's return

Hard to imagine it, lying intact,
folded into books: identity
to be assumed like tartan,
or spelt out on museum clocks
from heretic stones and peat-blacked pots,
history by strip light. Do we know
where we are in these tourist hills?
Is it plantain we chew to draw the taste
our childhood was? The soft, even names
come easily, we have the voice for them, we know
the stories of threadwork and burning turf
and supple hands that gather in a storm.
And when we reach the narrow, choppy loch
we remember the legends of giant fish
that no one believed and everybody told
as we drove south that morning, years ago,
pretending we could find our own way home.

Personal

1

It's an old room full of beautiful junk,
street signs, picture books and wooden keys,
and you're the only one who finds things there.

It's an old room with voices in the walls
and cypress at the window full of owls;
an old room smelling of paint and polished steel,
semi-precious, steadfast, incomplete.

No one you could ever show it to:
your largest burden and your last defence
is this one confidence you have to keep,
these clockwork toys and rabbit skulls in jars.

It's an old room with a door you leave unlocked,
a blue and yellow room, with broken chairs,
and needles on the floor, from Christmas trees.

2

There is a place in sleep, you hold it
like the locked space inside a tabernacle
filled with the radio sounds of childhood,
the grass-bitters taste of infatuations
you never outgrew, but packed away like old
certificates or school reports. You kept
saying you'd come again, and it's true:
there's always a rendezvous to keep
on this veranda, and a kitchen light
burning when the rest have gone to bed,
where you sit drinking coffee from a pot
you threw out years ago, you never guessed
you had kept it, brand new, for nights like this.

Keeping secret

In those days I listened at doors
and everything ran through my hands, unused,

like water. In those days I held the belief
that some things were never discussed,

like money, or love.
Whenever a silence fell I knew it was there

for a purpose. In those days I thought
everyone played by the rules,

and I was alone, like a spy, my ear to the door,
or hidden amidst the bracken, sick with surprise,

watching a stranger do terrible things in the shadows.

Clarity

How I stood by the window
and wanted things exact
like the wide sky over a hockey field
or the lane to the teaching college
when dead leaves rose in the wind
and followed like flat birds.

And how I liked reading in catalogues
of crystal and aquatints
and lilies shaped from porcelain
centuries ago. I found it
hanging in the dark, a shook
curtain of snow and stars
and the hill paths ringing.

But even at its most precise
I lost it, like the times
I cracked a sherbet lemon in my teeth
and the tang filled my throat
a moment only. Afterwards
the same plain taste of myself, a lukewarm
fabric of milk and wool, and nothing sure.

Brother

You were dead in the womb. They had to cut you loose:
like some diver trapped in a wreck
you lay helpless, tethered to death
by the cord. We hated you for that.

The flowers in a jar
by Mother's bed:
narcissi and hazel twigs.
A kind of sign.

I remember the dreams I had about that time:
the milk in my glass transformed to blood
and still I drank it,
thirsting in your place.

You grew beside me steadily,
your mass and volume echoed in my own.
At night you lay against me in a thick
gossamer of cries.

And once I heard your name.
I always thought you had preceded me;
like any aboriginal, you played
hide and seek with souls.

My only magic, sharp and hard
like a bone in my locked throat,
I wanted you to catch me unawares,
to step into my shoes and walk away.

Two saints

My first school was a wooden bungalow
named for Brigid, patron saint of wells.
I thought she must be cold, like the closed spring
that whispered in the wood behind our house,
but later I was told of sacred fires
deep in Kildare, where monasteries were built
according to Pope Gregory's decree.
The elder Brigid glimmered in that land:
a motion under flames, the shifting greens
of dark and bright, bound in a speaking hearth.
I felt time shatter when the Normans came.

Lessons went unlearned. I played a part,
scratched the twelve times table on my cuffs
and copied spelling lists from hidden books.
But I was thinking of the undergrowth.
There would be dreams and Brigid would be there;
blue as rain her firelight on my skin.

One day I helped my father clear a pond.
We drew rakes through the water, gathered weed
and raised it dripping, shot with sudden light.
The weft was heavy, tugging for its depth.
Spread on the path, it shone like new-dyed silk.

That year we moved. There was another school:
red brick walls, locks and window bars.
It echoed like a vault when we ran out
to Christmases; the waxy corridors
swarmed with Roman numerals and names.
Saint Columba's High. If there were tales
of wicker furnaces and holy wells
I have forgotten them.
Every month we had a class exam:
History was statute books and wars,
Sixteen Hundred to the present day,
never reaching now. I started French.
All I knew of that school's saint was this:

that it was he who gave the people
books and silence at the story's end
and on an island sheltered from the stream
he drowned the oracles in chiselled stone.

A death in the family

To take a book down from the topmost shelf
and turn the pages:
the stillness of a hunting ocelot,
a map of India with chiming names.

The room might smell of ink or Ovaltine
and no sound but the rain.
You might have come in misty from the storm,
you might have heard the voices in the hall

but you are neutral. Nobody expects
a child to understand.
Though you have read such things in magazines,
and later, when they come and go all night

– the men in overcoats, with leather bags
and pearled umbrellas –
you know, but you pretend you cannot know
and close the book. That jungle disappears.

Silentium

Quick snow piled against the hut door
and your wireless behind the net
window, keeping its own counsel.
I wanted to be like that: alone
and listening, on winter afternoons,
while evening crept from the fields
and hedges. When they called me in,
I would sit by the grate, silently
huddled, like someone guarding
a thin yellow flame, and later,
lifting the scuttle and stepping out,
I would stand in the dark a moment,
the scullery glow at my back
and my face to the wind.

Fetching sloes

The childhood pride that I had names for things
and carried signs beneath my fingernails
and in my shoes; the quiet of the woods
draped around me at the kitchen door
when I came home, reluctantly, to bed.
The knowledge of an undergrowth, and codes
I never learned,
the confidence of hidden animals
– it all returns when we go out for sloes,
carrying them back in plastic bags
and standing in the scullery for hours,
washing, pricking, sneaking sips of gin,
the bright, dark juice uncurling from our hands.

Self-

The smell on my hands was sure,
but names were all deceit, and feel
slid beneath my fingers like the sheer
silk of mother's shawl.

Although the mirror watched me when I moved –
a sinking sand, or needle's eye of love
that nobody could pass –

I never failed in peeling from the glass
a look I could outface:
as if one glance was more than I could lose,
illusion there more self than all I was.

Anamnesis

Memory, you should have known,
is a double agent:

one of those gaberdine
people in films, a smiling

Harry Lime. It leads you
through scalars and cosines

to the murmur of cuckoo clocks.
It leads you

into a sewer. You strike
matches and the rats

squeal. Up ahead
someone is splashing away

through grey water. A hurried
figure you know from somewhere,

splashing and stumbling
into the flashlights and guns.

The quest

1

You begin with the fauna you invent.
Like Adam, waking in a certain world,
looking, talking. Nothing is not your own,
nothing is itself till it is found.
Then you are deceived by otherness:
the treason of a flame, or holly leaves,
the grip of ice. Perhaps you muddle through,
dismayed, mistrustful, ready to deny;
perhaps you choose the easy presences,
filling the world with names, for naming's sake,
and finishing with paradise refused:
improbable dark shapes and secret beasts
abandoned in the ringwork of the Tree
when Adam spoke, and knew what he had lost.

2

We grew up believing in such a place:
a wounded king in the mist, a red fox
leading the hero to a holy spring.
We entered by the snow, the holly grove
was full of thrushes, evening arrived
through smoke. We grew remembering
another country, happy sentiments
whistled between the scratches on 78s.
And who would deny the small epiphanies
of Sunday afternoons, the jerseys
streaming for a try, or hymns,
meaningless and strong, around our fire?
We did no harm. And if we missed the Grail
some other, safer prize could still be won.

3

This could be the Grail myth where the hero
cannot be lost; his pledge is to survive.
The wheel may roll him back into the dust
remorselessly; the sun may raise him up,
breathing in damp clay and sickening
for the pure violence of angels. This
is simple history and fairy tale
repeated, known by heart, unverified.
In any story book, an errant knight
may walk among the beasts and learn to wake
the dragon sleeping under earth's black wires.
We are confirmed by legends we forget
and every vessel is the one true Grail,
unnoticed, rusting, irreplaceable.

4

I rise in the waxen dark. The snow
is steady and exact, with time enough
to fill the city. Out beyond the park
sirens are muffled, an incident
assumed into the lights, each casualty
a splinter of the possible. Tonight
I track a shadow to my window pane,
a tiger with my smile who scents a kill
among the travellers on exit roads.
But living has become a testament
to prey I did not take and ventures wrapped
in careful flesh. A fear of accidents;
new snowfalls leaving tripwires in my path,
the vertigo of finding my own depth.

5

Winter fixes us in history:
the sparrowhawk a signal in his tight
murderous hover; trees defined as light,
like fallen angels buried in a well,
harnessed to their secrets. After rain
the fields are empty and the wood is full
of talking animals and golden
pomegranates ripened out of season.
Look, we can see a journey from this train:
the strong, deceitful knight rides out to seek
his Avalon; the Green Man bares his neck.
Spawn-coloured water spends in the ploughshare's wake
and Spring runs after, bleeding from the steel,
a fisher's wound that time declines to heal.

'Only the rain'

Only the rain takes this road
from Uley to Cam,
rain, and the weight of horses,
a rattle of empty churns
and the moon's wet tracks.
Perhaps we dream of walking
between these fields:
a dog barks from the lane,
somebody stands at a gate
in the first green of day.
And sometimes we think ourselves here
with time stopped, and parallel hedges
steeped in woodsmoke and dusk.
But only the rain takes this road
from Uley to Cam,
rain, and a flicker of stars
on the rim of each pail.

The bounds

1

There is a danger here:
herons wading in the first light
on smoky waters
after those stories you heard, of fishermen
hauled into the dark on their own lines;

a danger in the woodbine and the rose
and those moss-water pools in alder woods,
brackish and sexual; there is

a danger, when you do collaborate;
lizards and horses populate your dreams
and messages arrive: November winds
shaking the doors, a rush of wings, the wild
speech of a house you knew before the fall.

2

It is a notion of the holy ground:
a saint's land, the scarcer ferns
and orchids of legend;
white bulls standing in the narrow lanes;
those evening fires
kindled in hoops; a sodden fleece
of watchers near the well;
purple and sage-coloured rags
on hazel boughs. It is
invisible on maps, a driver's
rainwater vision:
October hills, the gold of brackens;
minute by minute, the steady dark
seeping in to fill the service trees.

3

The old names on the old maps,
lists where we find our own words tucked away
into the language of strangers.
Imagination fills those parishes,
raising Downham Hill above a yard
where herds like this one struggle for milking
into the same smell, the same hard voices.
Evening arrives like a flock of starlings
here and then; we have another
village at the lane's end, yellow lamps
in limestone windows and a snow
that only falls in maps, filling the space
between the hedges and the sable lanes.

All Hallows at Newbrook Farm

A premise of autumn's logic:
three in the afternoon, the raw milk
standing on the table, and
windows dark with rain.
The clock walks up and down the stairs
folding moths in the curtains,
and we find beetle cases, empty of ticking,
behind the chairs. Outside,
beyond the Thuja hedge, beyond the walls,
sleek-furred rabbits crouch inside the hill
and foxes observe a season of hunger
echoed in bells
and the silence of Kilner jars.
The conversation dies. No privacy
where we still feel the anger of the dead,
their lifelong fears and unfinished gestures
stacked against the doors
like bales of wool.

After the harvest

A flower arranger's season:
teasel heads and heps
and lapwing fields.

An open door. A broom.
A jug of milk.
Puddles of olive shade
in the sunlit room.

We live for the shuck of corn,
for purple berries
bleeding on the thorn,

the blue spire in the valley,
woodsmoke and starling wires,
the hoop of the people, gathered anew
in the glimmer of autumn fires.

Green

Take it as a guide, this thread
of river weed: its smell, its feel.
Moving inward through the labyrinth,

follow, where it breaks and is resumed
beneath a stone in whited leaves of grass
or on the fen road, where a watersplash

decides your course. For something draws you in:
you find the centre of the mazy grain
and start afresh. The shaping of a world

is in your hands. You have to make it green.

An English Suite

1. *On Merrow Down*

This is the moment of the cuckoo bee,
lurching from bullace to cardamine;
heat bleeds the trees; Brimstone and Orange Tip
wink in the plaited grass; the meadow stands
in the pool of its own shade, summer-stunned,
even the dowsing beetle, on a spiked
acre of Yorkshire Fog, is heron-like,
wading in fleece; stopped rabbits dream of air,
pressed to their pulsing young, terrified, live
scent maps of fox paths and snares;
the little owl waits in the lucid roof,
above the lunchtime walkers, to descend
through the cool stratus of an evening wind
into the hoop of rain and yellow stars.

2. *The seaside buses*

I remember the pineapple weed
beside the road, and ribbons
of spindrift sand. My silhouette
would burn for miles on the gold haze,
bruising the driver's window.
Squat houses stood by the road
and children ran out to wave.
That was where summer lived: when I stepped
down from the oak-floored bus
new people came to meet me
with peaches and ninety-nines, and time
waded the heaven of rock-pools,
a stranded merman, waiting for the tide.

3. *Fen colours*

The way the eye is casually seduced
by flatness, or the lonely petrol lights
on moonlit roads,

or how you always end by driving
out, through purple suburbs, to a blue
of pasture land or sea,

having to carry the pink of lupins
for miles, or find a cipher for the reek
of leafsmoke in your coat.

The way you reduce what you can to a clean
ideogram: the wind, the colour green,
and how you return

with nothing, or next to nothing and a feel
for less: the pregnant pause, the unpursued.

4. *A calendar for the parish of Bagpath*

As if those names worked here:
the pharisaic, tallow-measured
stations of a year; yellow and black
scarabs in an almanac; enforced
vigils and feasts. At times
blank pages are our saints' days:
clapping bells, a stillness by the walls,
alders smudged with rain.
And meaning is local: perhaps
we come home and empty boxes,
letters, locomotives, daisy chains
are spread across the floor, old schemes
knitting, like a web of medick stems,
or we are double agents all the time:
cheerful pagans, flocking to the church
at Candlemas, to cherish Brigid's flame.

5. *At Owlpen*

Pigeons stand for angels in this dream
of England. Sunday stones and windfalls
are chapters in a Book of Revelation
left open on the altar after Mass.

Old names peel away under the moss;
there is a music in the narrow woods
and over the ploughed fields a ceaseless
rushing of wings. Children go silently

into their chambers of milk and lichen,
leaving a country we know from old prints:
avenues of beech and royal choirs,

oak leaves and yellow roofs, the parishes
that nobody has seen, though they were real
for one bright evening when the hedges burned.